CHIHULY

CHIHULY

at the VIRGINIA MUSEUM OF FINE ARTS

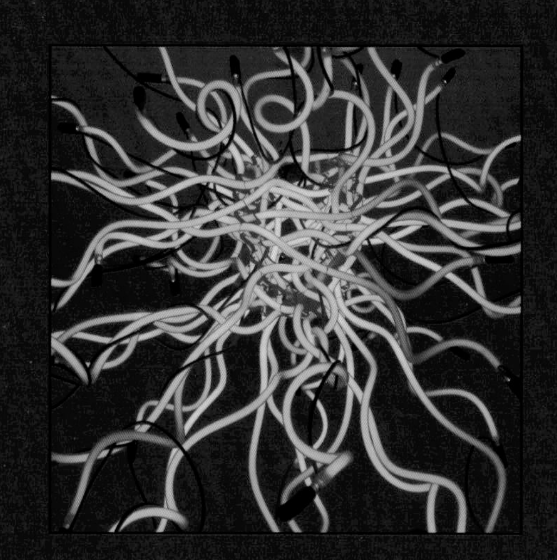

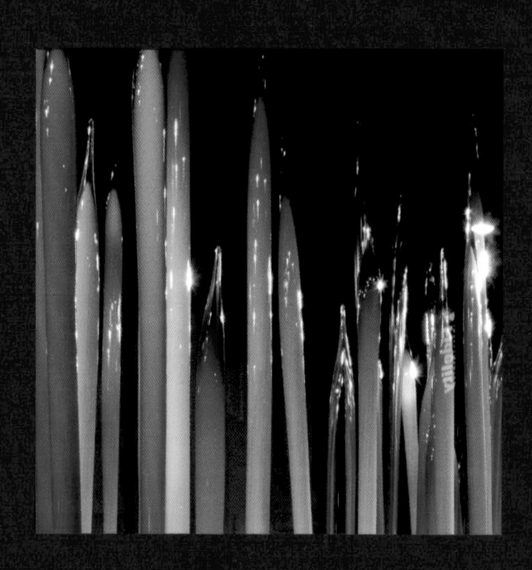

CHIHULY

at VMFA

Chihuly at the Virginia Museum of Fine Arts is the internationally renowned glass artist's third major U.S. museum exhibition in recent years, following efforts that drew record-breaking crowds at the de Young Museum in San Francisco in 2008 and the Museum of Fine Arts, Boston, in 2011. From bold flowers to architectural installations around the world, in historic cities, public museums, and gardens, Chihuly has revolutionized the studio glass movement and elevated the medium of glass from the realm of craft to fine art.

Chihuly continues to expand the technical and virtuoso possibilities of glass as a medium. The VMFA exhibition includes many of Chihuly's iconic works—*Ikebana, Mille Fiori, Chandeliers, Tabac Baskets, Boats, Persian Ceiling*—as well as site-specific installations, taking advantage of the museum's McGlothlin Wing with its 12,000-square-foot special exhibition galleries, soaring atrium, and reflecting pools. The exhibition is a wonderful complement to our 2011 exhibition, *Tiffany: Color and Light,* which explored the work of another great master of glass.

An undertaking of this scope and ambition involves many hands. Of course, we want to thank Dale Chihuly and the entire Team Chihuly—especially Britt Cornett, Head of Exhibitions, and Vice President Billy O'Neill—an amazingly professional and creative group of individuals. It has been a pleasure and a privilege to work with them all.

At VMFA the project director of the exhibition was Robin Nicholson, Deputy Director for Art and Education, assisted by Exhibition Coordinator Courtney Burkhardt. Curatorial oversight was provided by Barry Shifman, Lewis Family Curator of Decorative Arts, 1900–Present. Design, installation, security, and many other matters were overseen by Stephen Bonadies, Deputy Director for Collections and Facilities Management, working with the Head of Design, Doug Fisher; Registrars Susan Turbeville and Karen Daly; and the Head of Exhibition Production, Bob Francis. The marketing and communication plan was organized and managed by Director of Marketing Bob Tarren, with the support of the world-acclaimed Richmond-based Martin Agency. Budget management fell under the purview of Fern Spencer, Chief Financial Officer; Anne Kenny-Urban, Manager of Budget Services; and Aiesha Halstead, Manager of Exhibitions. The accompanying educational programs were organized by Trent Nicholas and Courtney Morano. The impressive fundraising campaign to support Chihuly at VMFA was overseen by Linda Lipscomb, Deputy Director for Advancement, and her team. This publication was designed by Sarah Lavicka, Chief Graphic Designer, with a personal essay by our colleague at Virginia Commonwealth University, Dr. Robert Hobbes. The stunning image of Chihuly's installation in VMFA's reflecting pool was taken by Travis Fullerton, Museum Photographer.

I hope you enjoy this publication, which documents a truly once-in-a-lifetime exhibition by a great American artist.

ALEX NYERGES
Director

Meeting

CHIHULY

Dale Chihuly and I first met at a small dinner in La Jolla, California, in the summer of 1983, hosted by his long-term close friend, the Italian sculptor, ceramicist, and glass artist Italo Scanga. At the time, Chihuly's *Cylinders, Baskets,* and *Seaforms* were beginning to be noticed by members of the art world, who recognized these series of glass objects to be among the first to cross the imagined divide separating fine craft from art. My initial interest in Chihuly began with a little-known but important 1971 collaboration he had undertaken with James Carpenter, when the two of them had created at the Rhode Island School of Design (RISD) the stirring minimalist installation *20,000 Pounds of Ice and Neon.* It had been undertaken two years after Chihuly had established the eminent RISD glass program and only three years after he had made a name for himself in the American studio glass movement as the first American glass-blower to work in the renowned Venini factory on the Venetian island of Murano.

When we met, I had just completed the five-stop European tour of my retrospective exhibition on earth artist Robert Smithson, which had been selected as the United States' official entry for the 1982 Venice Biennale. Although famous for his *Spiral Jetty* in the Great Salt Lake in Utah, Smithson had also been intrigued with low-temperature physics and with crystallography, particularly with the ways crystals can appear to grow, thereby appearing to bridge the enormous gap separating the physical and biological sciences. Smithson was captivated by the essential contradiction represented by glass, which looks crystalline, when it is in fact on the molecular level a frozen liquid and thus structurally chaotic. Chihuly's *20,000 Pounds of Ice and Neon,* an assembly of colored neon tubes frozen in large cubes of ice, covering an area of 600 square feet and allowed to thaw as an integral part of the work's performance, encapsulated and heightened the ensuing contradictions between the two frozen liquids of glass and ice, representing respectively hot and cold temperatures, as well as manufactured and natural materials. Although unintended as an extension of Smithson's ideas, Chihuly and Carpenter's installation served as a wonderful pendant to this New York artist's eight-foot-long *Glass Stratum* (1967), which is comprised of stacked layers of emerald green industrial glass, making his completed assembly resemble a frozen crystalline waterfall.

That first night at Italo's dinner we discussed Smithson's work, Chihuly's brief foray into minimalism, his love of American Indian art, continued ties with the West Coast, particularly his home in Seattle and childhood in nearby Tacoma, as well as his great ambition to take the art of the all-important twentieth-century Venetian master Paolo Venini, known for working with cutting-edge designers and architects, in the direction of a distinctly American aesthetic by making it larger, more closely connected with nature than with fashion, and much more highly keyed.

A couple of years after our meeting, one of Dale Chihuly's many assistants telephoned to ask if I would consider writing a piece on Dale's *Macchia* series, which had been initiated around the time we met and which Italo Scanga in fact had named.[1] Although employing an Italian word for an American glass series might appear an affectation, Dale liked the ability of the term *macchia* to encapsulate and characterize his spontaneous way of working. Derived from the Latin *macula, macchia* might connote simply a stain or a spot, but since the time of the Renaissance, it has been associated in artistic circles with a sketchy way of applying initial color to a drawing or painting. A particularly appropriate word for the late style of the Venetian painter Titian, *macchia* has been used to characterize this master's emphasis on brushwork and summary treatment of form. In the seventeenth century, *macchia* was employed to designate the ways improvisational sketches can appear to be nature's miraculous creation rather than the work of human hands. Two centuries later, moving away from the work of art to its creator, *macchia* came to signify the artist's first mental and/or visual insight, which usually serves as the focus of an initial sketch. This later, highly romantic definition, with its emphasis on artists' ability to reveal their special sensibilities as embodiments of their own specific and unique natures, served in fact as the name for the group of painters known as the Macchiaioli, who were the French Impressionists' Italian counterparts.

After I agreed to write about this new series of works, Dale's assistant asked if I had ever witnessed one of his glassblowing sessions, which even at that time had become legendary. Since I had not, I was encouraged to fly to Seattle and accompany Dale on his next session at the Pilchuck Glass School, which he had founded soon after RISD's program, so that I might see him in action. Since losing the use of one eye and with it the necessary depth perception to blow glass, Dale, who always appeared roguishly dressed with a distinguished and distinguishing black patch over his nonfunctional eye, had emphasized his role as idea person and impresario. While the Pilchuck glass shop was being readied for action, Dale sat nearby, concentrating on a series of generous, quickly conceived drawings he wanted to serve as guides. Swiftly composing with a fistful of colored pencils, sometimes as many as a dozen in all grasped in one hand, Dale would draw broad and sweeping, incredibly organic and lyric shapes, which were then punctuated with dilated openings to suggest palpitating living forms, which his then-favored glassblower William Morris would undertake to realize. Later that day, whenever Morris reached the strategic moment when the mottled huge bubbles of glass would look as if they were about to explode, Chihuly would come on stage. Working with one or two water-soaked fruit paddles to keep them from burning, he would begin a brief yet all-important commandeering dance with the glass, while Morris continued holding it with the glassblower's pipe. At this point Dale Chihuly was able to endow each piece with its unique organic shape, thus ensuring that the work bore his own indelible stamp. Enormously generous and playful, even though he was obviously incredibly serious about his art, Chihuly worked to keep up the spirits of his entire crew by arranging for an ever-present spread of food and snacks, always accompanied by lively music, so the glassblowing sessions, for all their intensity, resembled large ongoing parties.

Because I knew Dale to be enormously close to his mother, who continued to live in Tacoma in the house in which he had grown up, I asked to be introduced to her. After the intense session at Pilchuck, Dale and I returned that evening to Seattle; the next day we headed to Tacoma to meet his mother. The house was modest, as one might expect of a single parent who had the full responsibility of the family after the death of her husband, who had been a local butcher, but the garden beside it—obviously one of Mrs. Chihuly's great passions—was anything but modest. In fact the flowers in the garden appeared profligate, with riotously colored, dinner-plate-sized dahlias populating and overrunning this area, a great number standing five feet and even higher, looking more like the fantasy of a *Wizard of Oz* set designer than nature's work. Sumptuously vulgar and wonderfully monstrous in their uninhibited beauty, Mrs. Chihuly's prized dahlias were obviously a great inspiration for Chihuly's work, challenging him to find ways to transpose aspects of their blatant freshness into the many series that he has created over the past three decades. During this time, as Chihuly has continued to test himself by raising the ante with each new series, sometimes apparently in emulation of his mother's garden even to the point of planting his proliferating glass pieces in parks and pools of water to create over-the-top installations, causing some critics to regard him as the glass world's Jeff Koons, I often think of Mrs. Chihuly's intensely hued, prized giant dahlias with their wide-spread blossoms, sometimes as large as a foot in diameter.

ROBERT HOBBS
The Rhoda Thalhimer Endowed Chair of American Art
Virginia Commonwealth University

1. The following discussion is based on my essay "Reflections on Chihuly's *Macchia*" in Dale Chihuly, *Chihuly alla macchia* (Beaumont: Art Museum of Southeast Texas, 1993).

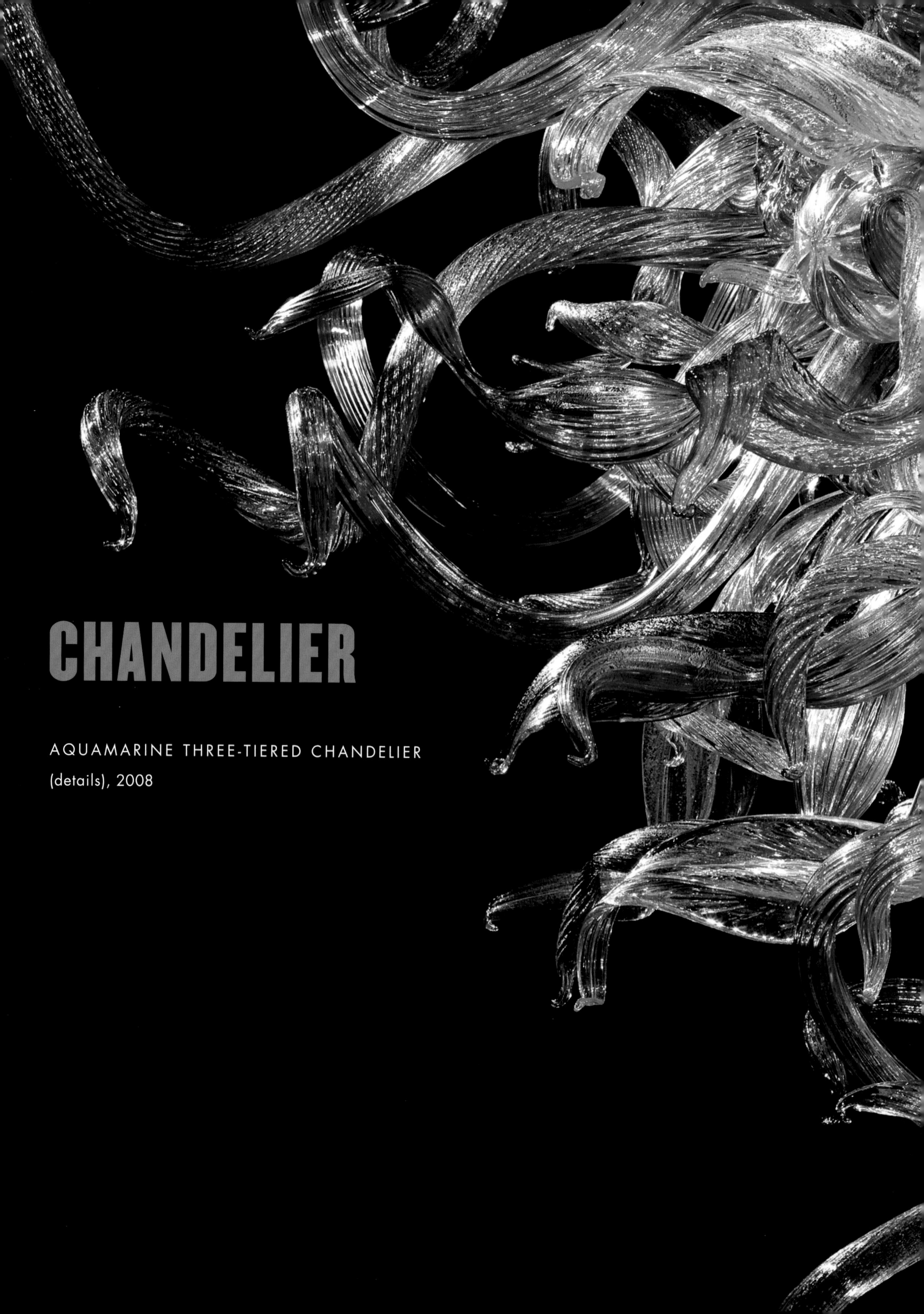

CHANDELIER

AQUAMARINE THREE-TIERED CHANDELIER
(details), 2008

BOATS and DRAWINGS

IKEBANA BOAT (details), 2008

FLOAT BOAT and IKEBANA BOAT, 2008

FLOAT BOAT, 2012

DRAWING WALL, 2008

DRAWINGS, 2009, 2007

PERSIAN CEILING

PERSIAN CEILING, 2002

PERSIAN CEILING (details), 2002, 2008

NORTHWEST ROOM

TABAC BASKETS (detail), 2007

TABAC BASKETS, 2008

TABAC BASKET SETS with DRAWING SHARDS and OXBLOOD BODY WRAPS, 2008

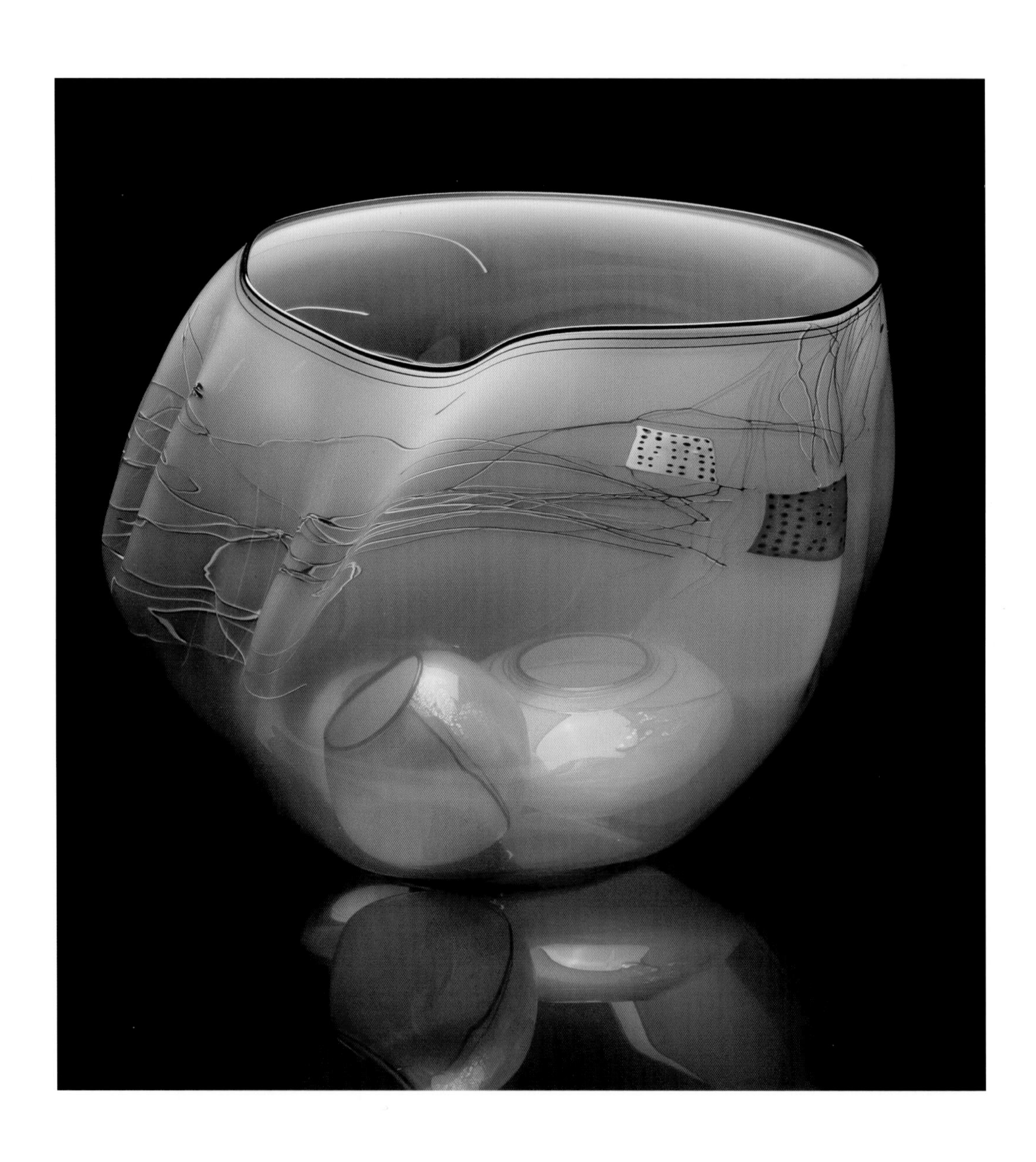

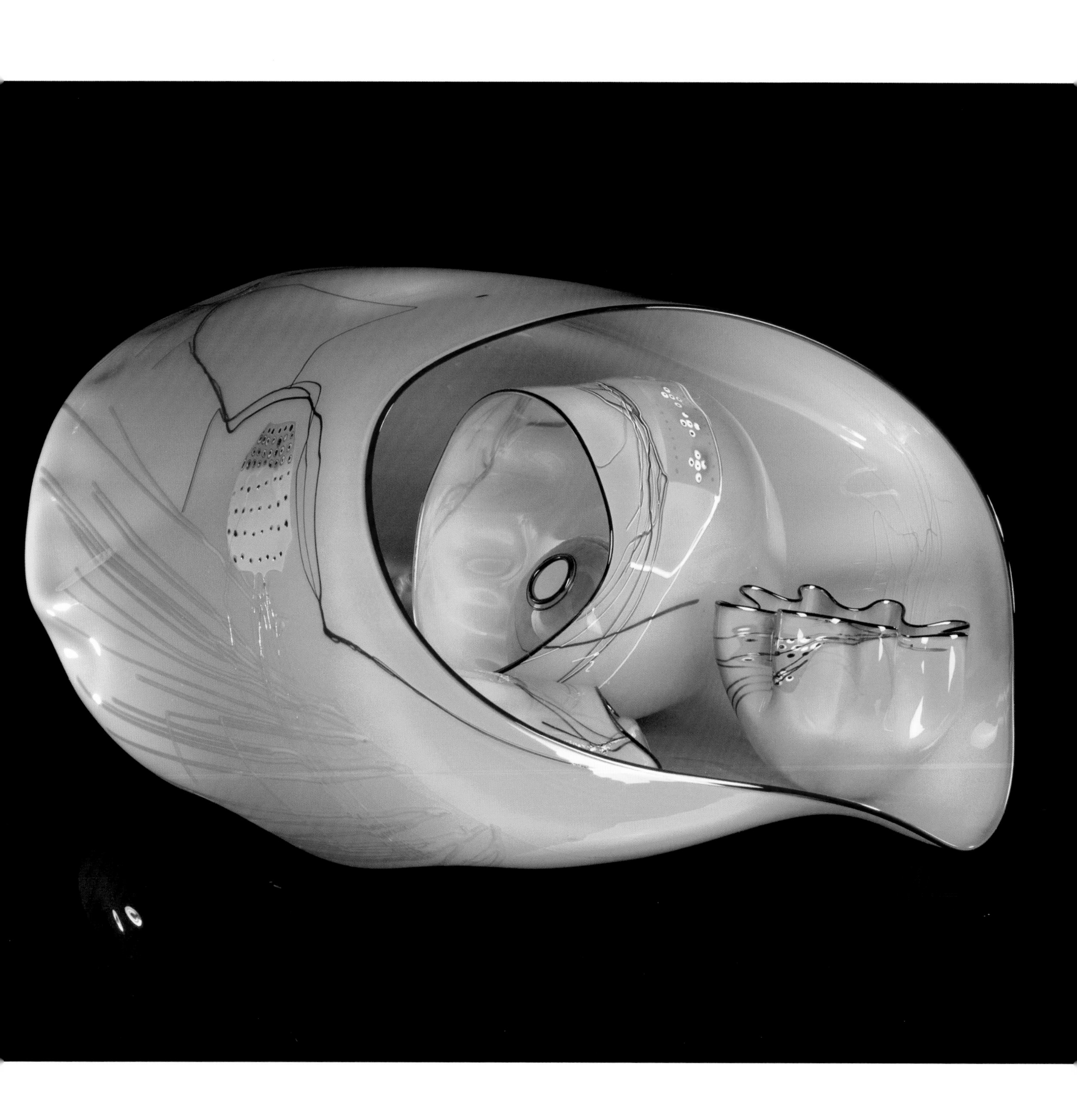

MACCHIA FOREST

MACCHIA FOREST (full view and detail), 2008

MACCHIA FOREST, 2012

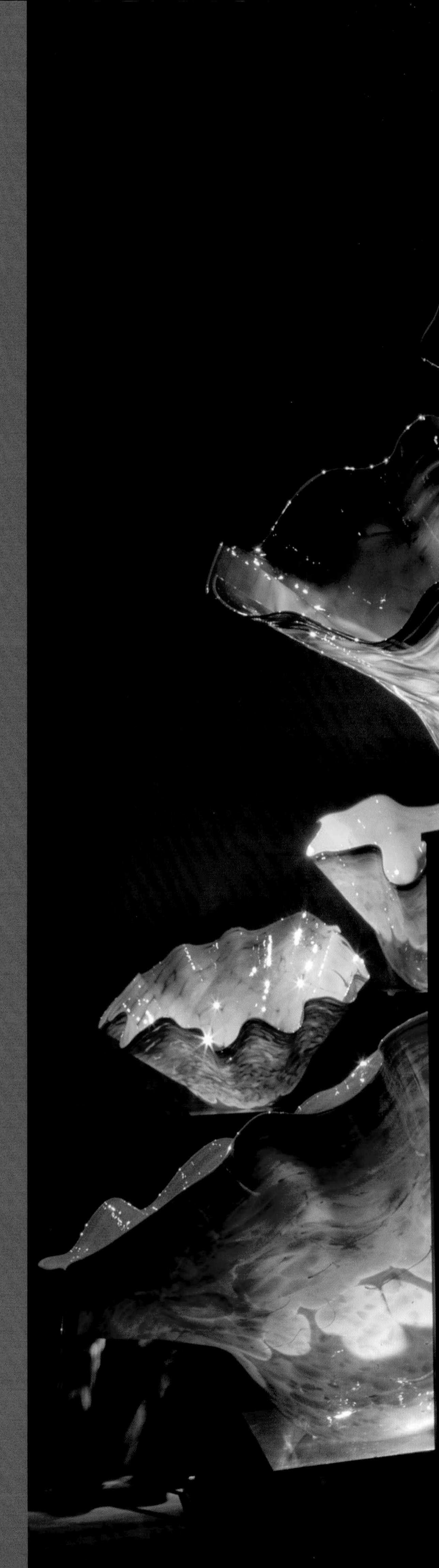

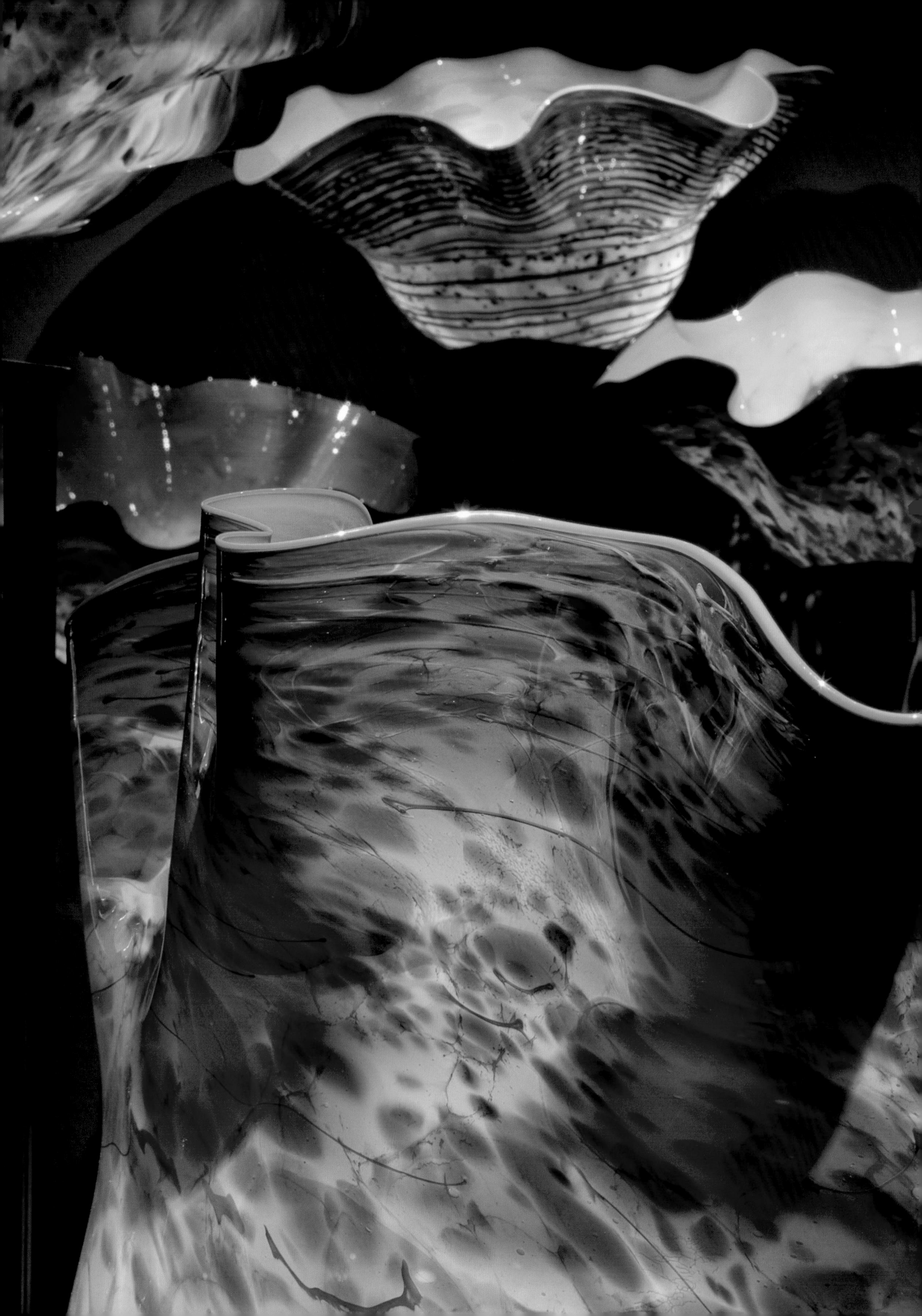

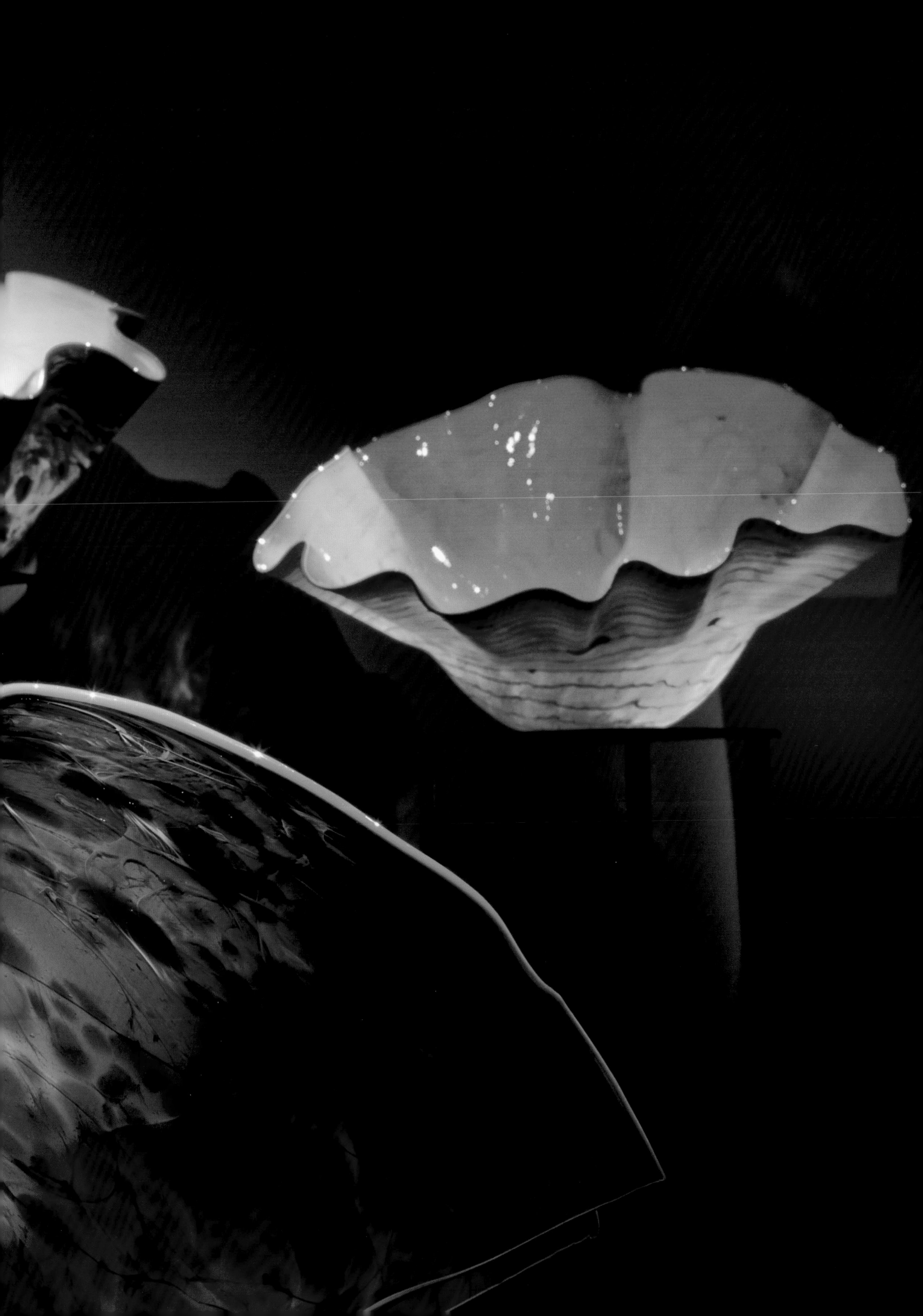

MILLE FIORI

MILLE FIORI (detail and full view), 2012

TUMBLEWEED

BLUE NEON TUMBLEWEED (full view and detail), 2010

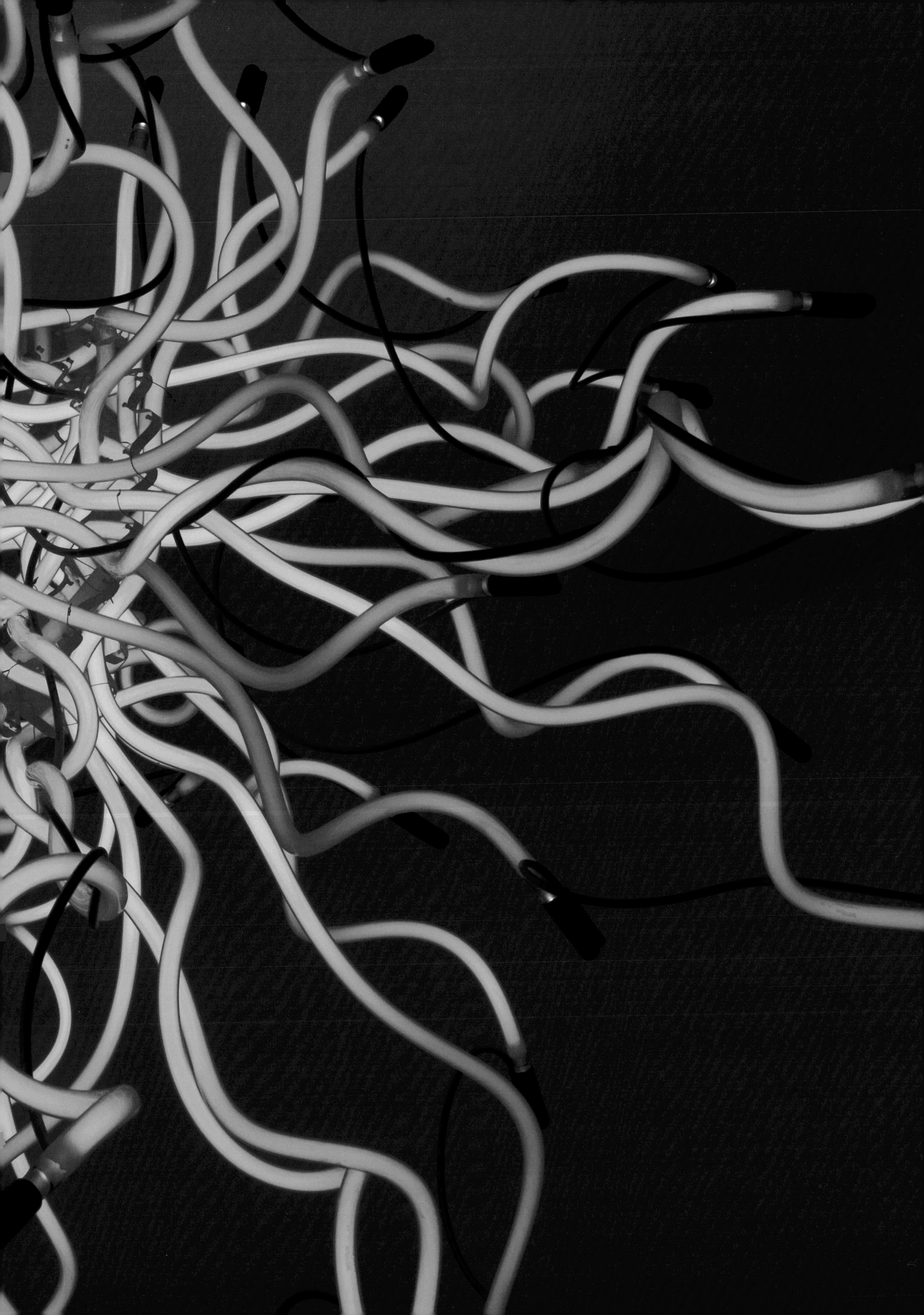

REEDS

BLUE REEDS (detail), 2010

REEDS and LOGS, 2008

DALE CHIHULY with TUMBLEWEED

Tacoma, Washington, 1993

ILLUSTRATIONS

Each installation or display of Dale Chihuly's works is unique to the environment in which it is placed. With the exception of the image of *Red Reeds* on the foldout and *Mille Fiori* on pages 48–51, the images in this catalogue were taken from similar but earlier installations.

Dust jacket front
Red Reeds (detail), 2007
Photo by: Jack Crane

Dust jacket back
Float Boat (detail), 2008
Photo by: Terry Rishel

pp. 2–4
Red Reeds, Virginia Museum of Fine Arts, Richmond, 2012
Photo by: Travis Fullerton

pp. 6–8, left to right:
Aquamarine Three-Tiered Chandelier (detail), Legion of Honor, San Francisco, 2008, 15 x 7½ x 7½ ft.
Photo by: Terry Rishel

Ikebana Boat (detail), 2008
Photo by: Scott M. Leen

Persian Ceiling (detail), Oklahoma City Museum of Art, Oklahoma City, Oklahoma, 2002, 40 x 6 ft.
Photo by: Terry Rishel

Tabac Basket Set with Drawing Shards and Oxblood Body Wraps, 2008, 7 x 18 x 20 in.
Photo by: Scott M. Leen

Macchia Forest, de Young Museum, San Francisco, 2008
Photo by: Terry Rishel

Mille Fiori (detail), Virginia Museum of Fine Arts, 2012
Photo by: Nathaniel Willson

Blue Neon Tumbleweed, Morean Arts Center, St. Petersburg, Florida, 2010, 6 x 7 x 7 ft.
Photo by: Terry Rishel

Reeds and Logs (detail), Seattle, 2008, 8 x 35 x 14 ft.
Photo by: Terry Rishel

CHANDELIER

pp. 14–17
Aquamarine Three-Tiered Chandelier (details), Legion of Honor, San Francisco, 2008, 15 x 7½ x 7½ ft.
Photos by: Terry Rishel

BOATS and DRAWINGS

pp. 19 and 22–23
Ikebana Boat (details), 2008
Photos by: Scott M. Leen

pp. 20–21
Float Boat and **Ikebana Boat,** 2008
Photo by: David Emery

pp. 24–25
Float Boat (detail), *Chihuly Garden and Glass,* Seattle, 2012
Photo by: Terry Rishel

pp. 26–27
Drawing Wall, 2008
Photo by: Terry Rishel

p. 28
Baskets Drawing, 2009, 30 x 22 in.
Photo by: Charlie Wilkins

p. 29
Burned Black Ikebana Drawing, 2007, 30 x 22 in.
Photo by: Teresa Nouri Rishel

PERSIAN CEILING

pp. 30–31 and 35
Persian Ceiling, Oklahoma City Museum of Art, Oklahoma City, Oklahoma, 2002, 40 x 6 ft.
Photo by: Terry Rishel

pp. 32–33 and 34
Persian Ceiling (details), 2002, 2008
Photos by: Teresa Nouri Rishel

NORTHWEST ROOM

p. 37
Tabac Baskets (detail), 2007
Photo by: Terry Rishel

pp. 38–39
Tabac Baskets, de Young Museum, San Francisco, 2008
Photo by: Teresa Nouri Rishel

p. 40
Tabac Basket Set with Drawing Shards and Oxblood Body Wraps, 2008, 12 x 15 x 14 in.
Photo by: Scott M. Leen

p. 41
Tabac Basket Set with Drawing Shards and Oxblood Body Wraps, 2008, 7 x 18 x 20 in.
Photo by: Scott M. Leen

MACCHIA FOREST

pp. 42–45
Macchia Forest (full view and detail), de Young Museum, San Francisco, 2008
Photos by: Terry Rishel

pp. 46–47
Macchia Forest, *Chihuly Garden and Glass,* Seattle, 2012
Photo by: Scott M. Leen

MILLE FIORI

pp. 49–51
Mille Fiori (detail and full view), 2012
Photos by: Nathaniel Willson

TUMBLEWEED

pp. 53–55
Blue Neon Tumbleweed (full view and detail), Morean Arts Center, St. Petersburg, Florida, 2010, 6 x 7 x 7 ft.
Photos by: Terry Rishel

REEDS

p. 57
Blue Reeds (detail), Cheekwood Botanical Garden and Museum of Art, Nashville, 2010
Photo by: Scott M. Leen

pp. 58–59
Reeds and Logs, Seattle, 2008, 8 x 35 x 14 ft.
Photo by: Terry Rishel

p. 61
Dale Chihuly with Tumbleweed
Tacoma, Washington, 1993
Photo by: Russell Johnson

This catalogue accompanies the exhibition
CHIHULY at the Virginia Museum of Fine Arts,
October 20, 2012, through February 10, 2013.

Presenting Sponsor

Published by the Virginia Museum of Fine Arts
working in collaboration with Chihuly Workshop

Designed by Sarah Lavicka
Composed in Adobe InDesign with Champion Liteweight and Futura Book
Printed on Sappi McCoy Silk by Worth Higgins & Associates, Inc., Richmond, Virginia

Library of Congress Cataloging-in-Publication Data
Chihuly : at the Virginia Museum of Fine Arts / VMFA. — 1 [edition].
pages cm
This catalogue was published to accompany the exhibition Chihuly at the Virginia Museum of Fine Arts, October 20, 2012, through February 10, 2013.
ISBN 978-1-934351-01-7 (alk. paper)
1. Chihuly, Dale, 1941– Exhibitions. 2. Glass art—United States—Exhibitions.
I. Chihuly, Dale, 1941– Works. Selections. II. Virginia Museum of Fine Arts.
NK5198.C43A4 2012
748.092—dc23 2012031353

VIRGINIA MUSEUM OF FINE ARTS
200 N. Boulevard
Richmond, Virginia 23220
www.VMFA.museum